Word Problems

Matthew Mahaney

Flirtation #13

salò press

The Inclusion Problem, The Food Web Problem, The Logic Problem, The Night Problem, The Plotting Problem, and *The Symbiosis Problem* were originally published by *Lillet Press. The Diagnosis Problem, The Coastal Problem, The Chorus Problem, The Thawing Problem,* and *The Tundra Problem* were originally published in *Wax Nine*

978-1-8383602-3-8

Printed and Bound by 4Edge

Cover design and layout by Salò Press
Cover image by Melissa Perrey
Food chain image: Freepik.com

Typeset by Andrew Hook

Published by:
Salò Press
85 Gertrude Road
Norwich
UK

editorsalòpress@gmail.com
www.salòpress.com

Contents

SAMPLE QUESTION 1

Read the following pair of sentences, then choose the best answer to the question.

A person starts to imitate a whisper.
A maze is where a minotaur haunts a myth.

What is the function of the second sentence?
A) It makes the first sentence true.
B) It makes the first sentence false.
C) It restates the same idea.
D) It gives an example.

The correct answer is E) All of the above.

SAMPLE QUESTION 2

Read the following passage, then choose the best answer to the question.

Maple seeds spin pink and yellow paper. Their wings are made of what maple is made of. They are different than a bee. They are different than a boy or girl or music. The sound of a maple seed is almost like paper, is almost like the word tree.

What is the main goal of this passage?
A) To entertain young children.
B) To help a reader who lacks imagination.
C) To provide an escape from reality.
D) To illustrate the values of a society.

The correct answer is E) None of the above.

The Brother Problem

Your brother's whisper envelops every fiber of your gaze. He codes an old example, then starts to sequence your flaws. When he tries to craft a proper clone, you fail to notice that his plan has shifted its posture. It glides a static angle, which causes you to miscount your breaths. What have you forgotten? How will you know when he cues the wrong release?

The Inclusion Problem

Use the information in the table to help you answer the question.

Number of Days Students Were Picked Up Early by a Parent During the School Year

	1 to 4	5 to 9	10 or more	Total
Group X	12	26	62	100
Group Y	63	22	15	100
Total	75	48	77	200

Group X consists of 100 children who have their own teacher, who go to the library instead of gym, who are late to school every morning, who wear the same hat every day, who get to ride in the elevator, who never notice their name being called, who draw the same field of flowers with markers in art, who leave early for lunch every day, who whisper into their hands, who pace and clap before leaving a room, who sometimes fall asleep in the sun at recess and miss the start of music class, who love to spin in their chairs, spin and spin and never get dizzy.

Group Y consists of 100 children who have brown eyes and are right-handed.

If a boy from Group X is placed in a new class, if he arrives with his name sewn onto a blue canvas bag, if he gets to play games on a laptop during silent reading time, if he leaves with a tall woman every Wednesday during math, if he wears special headphones that come in a rechargeable case, if he rocks and sucks his sleeve when he listens to music, if he hits himself in the head when he loses a game, when his headphones have not been recharged, when the wi-fi is down, when his words will not come, how long will it take for the other children to ask questions?

The Food Web Problem

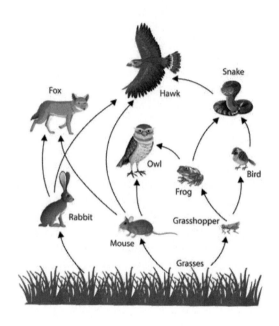

A food web is a system that absorbs a creature's death. A meadow can be a system if you recall the rain a claw collects, the wind and where it blooms, a single seed obscured by fur. If a rabbit misses when the silhouette of an owl avoids the moon, where does the energy in grasses go? Make a graph that shows how non-essential animals are ignored. Place an x beside the blooming spiral, then shade the section that reflects a fox's click.

The Conflict Problem

An army clogs a fleeting city. Their leader grieves a misheard order. He craves a static pasture, but his polished bluster yields an untenable array. Soon the shores are slick with floral oaths, with every soldier's semblance of a concentrated threat. If their retreat assumes a false composure, how many blooms will go unnoticed? What pretense should a poppy field exude?

The Partner Problem

The proper dress absolves a false persona. If skin and fur are each rehearsed, two girls will bloom a clone. Its stance is softly feral. The group of three constructs a new horizon with the grasses they obscure. Your task is gauging loss. Use your breath to mark the limits of a gulf. After averaging the absence, graph an orchid's ghost.

The Element Problem

A ratio of sadness exists in every atom. To find it, plot the points at which any orbit's aura is furthest from the moon.

The Diagnosis Problem

A new disease abounds. Doctors find its curdled sap in sinkholes in the brain. Further probes show a colony collapsed, as the mind becomes unkempt. Patients soon report having dreams where fire floats. How many memories will flash their redacted pollen in the time it takes a lipid to dissolve? At what point will a muddled brain become a berry soaked in ether?

The Coastal Problem

A woman drags her hands through silt. The cloud dispersed obscures her first impression, so she seeks a second prompt. She reminds herself that harbors can erode in southern spirals. She practices apologizing. As rust perfects a fence's abscess, the woman acquiesces to the fact that future algae will colonize her grave. If oil begins to blanket every gap in conversation, what frequency will best reduce a weather system's grief? To know this, first find the half-life of floral kelp on a foreign shore.

The Energy Problem

Two children share their oxygen in splashes. The alphabet they sing is how they know each other's name. High above them, the water locked inside a bee turns red as it beats a fevered map. The boys begin to argue over how to soothe the sun's confusion. Their phonic quarrel hovers, orange fur in little bursts above the water. How far from shore should they retreat to safely spend their sum?

The Thawing Problem

The warning of a frozen lake unspools in static bursts. Find the rate at which a mother's prayers are doubled. Use the outer edge of a broken thought to represent a forest's range.

The Chorus Problem

A girl is organizing every biome's music. She separates the notes for grass and knitted clover then primes a metronome with ice. Once she knows the radius of every hollow octave, she designates a fissure. An elegy unfolds. The muted cadence summons spores from every claw. At what point will migration be redundant? Which unfettered quadrant should the girl reclaim?

The Bayou Problem

For every egret's shadow that clashes with the skylight in a swamp, how many acres are added to the score a hatched cicada streams?

.

.

The Particulate Problem

Every seven seconds, a mollusk knits an atom. The surrounding static fish perceive this as gauze against their gills. A quantity of calcium is produced by this exchange. Were you to weigh it against a gram of marine snow, how many minutes would elapse before the moon began to groan?

The Ratio Problem

An unhatched creature feeds on tones. The sod appeases its nascent plea, and soon a beetle's glint is settled. It forages an axis. It collects a gold array. Remember that the Fibonacci sequence in a striated shell will refract an open octave. Knowing this, how can you predict when a splash of pollen will attack the thorax of a drone?

The Logic Problem

In a digital forest, owls are always floral. Floral owls never float. Mirrored owls float. Forests float. Pixels bloom. Pixels are always mirrored. Owls never bloom. Owls always mirror forests. Digital pixels are never floral. Floral pixels float. Some forests bloom floral mirrors.

Assume all of this is true.

How often do owls bloom pixels?
Would a mirrored forest bloom digital owls?

The Night Problem

Two girls are gathering shapes from the word *shadow*. They understand that any language needs a garden, so they scatter circles in perfect tandem. They make a kaleidoscope with seeds. When they aim it at the moon, they find a constellation that has never been named. One girl sees a hanging plant. The other, a handful of knives. Explain the girls' results, then sketch the sky they share.

The Process Problem

A boy is struggling to solve the string in his hands. His focus is unmoored by the way the wind reverses, by the errant tones rushing into the mouth of the cave his ear resembles. What steps should the boy take to unstick his sense of touch, to sort the information that has burrowed deeper than desired?

The Tundra Problem

If elk disperse their velvet in equivalent cocoons, how often have they stumbled in the taxidermied snow?

The Plotting Problem

A boy folds a map into a crooked cylinder then looks around for help. He's trying to find the area of a wilderness of wanting. He's been asked to graph a lake's desire to ferry a swan. He checks the clock again and wonders how to figure out why a storm returns a bell's recursive lull. Where should he begin? Which formula or rule could possibly apply to his bright, percussive panic?

The Symbiosis Problem

A tree rejects a paper hive. It drips from a branch like an axe wrapped in wool, as a graft of bark weaves itself into place. The evicted colony finds a lake of milk to infect. Unopened flowers rot on its shore. Graph the curve of a queen reclined, then predict the circumference of her first seven eggs. If each wax chalice remains intact, how many times can collapse be deferred?

The Perception Problem

Chloe only speaks in Sailor Moon. Her steady script is a comfort to others, a way to note the passing time and watch a scene unfold. One teacher says she wishes she could be as happy, that she's smarter than she looks, that her looping speech and sound effects reveal a deeper understanding than you would ever expect. She misses when another teacher bristles. If Chloe changes classes, how quiet will her new teacher need her script to stay? How often will she suggest a walk or office trip? How long before she asks if she might calm her constant hands?

Matthew Mahaney is also the author of *The Plural Space*, (Saló Press, 2016), *The Storm That Bears Your Name* (The Cupboard, 2015), and *Your Attraction to Sharp Machines* (BatCat Press, 2013). He earned his MFA at the University of Alabama and is currently a poetry fellow in the PhD program at the University of Louisiana-Lafayette.